JOURNEY
THROUGH
GRIEF

by

Elizabeth Brooks Farnsworth

Best wishes to Jennifer.
Elizabeth B Fn
10/22/86

Foreword by Elisabeth Kübler-Ross, M.D.

Epilogue by John David Smith, Ed.D.

SUSAN
HUNTER
Atlanta, Georgia

Published by Susan Hunter Publishing, Atlanta, Georgia.

Printed in the United States of America

5   4   3   2   1

Publisher: Susan Hunter
Editor: Phyllis Mueller
Illustrations: Judy Noyes-Farnsworth
Editorial Assistants: Allison Adams, Tamara Sokolec

Library of Congress Cataloging-in-Publication Data

Farnsworth, Elizabeth Brooks, 1952-
    Journey through grief / by Elizabeth Brooks Farnsworth; foreword by Elisabeth Kübler-Ross; epilogue by John David Smith.
        p.   cm.
    Bibliography: p. 81
    ISBN 0-932419-18-6
    1.   Farnsworth, Elizabeth Brooks, 1952-   . 2.   Down's syndrome—Psychological aspects. 3.   Mothers—United States—Biography. 4.   Grief. I.   Title.
RJ506.D68F37   1988
362.1'9892858842—dc19   88-818
[B]

Interested readers may write to the author at this address:

Elizabeth Brooks Farnsworth
c/o Susan Hunter Publishing
1447 Peachtree St., N.E.
Suite 807
Atlanta, GA 30309

CONTENTS

FOREWORD

Elizabeth Farnsworth's book, *Journey Through Grief*, should be read by every parent who has given birth to a child with special needs. It is a moving account of a couple whose second child was born with Down Syndrome and who after open-heart surgery and many ups and downs, hopes, and much despair, finally returned to his maker.

It is a book of courage, hope, and sharing, and will show others in grief that there are ways to make it bearable and — yes, eventually grow through all the pain and become more compassionate, understanding, and loving.

Elisabeth Kübler-Ross, M.D.

ACKNOWLEDGEMENTS

It is no easy task to acknowledge the many people who have contributed in some way to the life of this book.

I thank my husband, Dave, for his unending support of the project. He encouraged my efforts and wrote a computer program which provided a mechanism for me to store and amend my writing in an expedient manner. He listened to the frustrations I expressed when "writer's block" paralyzed my progress.

I thank my son, Michael, whose life and growth is a marvel to me. He taught me to love, irregardless of the labeling created by human beings. His purity of heart was a beacon in turbulent seas.

I thank Dr. Elisabeth Kübler-Ross for her endorsement of my book. Her teachings and writings have taught me to think in new ways—to see beauty in the carvings created by the windstorms of life.

My long-time friend and a professional educator, Janet Coiner, offered compassionate editorial feedback. Her comments helped me improve the delivery of my message. I will always cherish many special moments shared with her.

Dr. John David Smith, professor of education and human development at Lynchburg College and a special friend, reviewed my manuscript numerous times and made many excellent suggestions. His support over the months of writing and decision-making are deeply appreciated. I also thank him for writing the epilogue to this book.

There have been many friends, relatives, and professionals who gave of themselves during difficult times. To name them all is impossible. Some entered our lives in hospital corridors for only brief moments. I remember their faces, if not their names. Others, like John Stephenson, Tina Millard, Mary Gough, Gloria Smith, Toni Dolan, and Maurine Harrison opened their hearts and stayed when it would have been far easier to stay away.

I thank my sister-in-law, Judy Noyes-Farnsworth, for her artistic creations of our children which grace this book.

To all of you who read my poems and cried tears of recognition, thank you for letting me know that I reached you.

I acknowledge all my friends in the Lynchburg, Va. Chapter of Compassionate Friends who, by their presence and words in meetings, led me to see that we are never alone in heartache.

To my friends and colleagues at Central Virginia Community Services, thank you for allowing me to use my combination of education and experience to advocate for adults with mental retardation. All of you are a special blessing in my journey. I have learned that helping others is a gift to the giver, as well as the receiver.

Our parents and siblings have supported and loved us very much. We appreciate you and know that your load was difficult to bear, too. We love all of you.

Special thanks to the staff at Susan Hunter Publishing for their commitment and expertise which made this book a reality. I am grateful to Susan Hunter for her faith in the book. To my editor, Phyllis Mueller, I offer my gratitude for the numerous technical improvements she made. Many thanks also to Beth Pearce, Billie Mears, and Carol Miller for the marketing and public relations work. All of you have been delightful to work with.

Last, but not least, I thank Thomas for his presence in my life. He had an impact on many lives, and I, for one, am not satisfied to allow his being to be used as a crutch for lifelong heartache. He taught me to cry out in agony—then, he led me to smell the air from atop the highest mountain, to rise above the hurt—never to forget, rather to BECOME.

Elizabeth Brooks Farnsworth
Lynchburg, Virginia

With love to
Dave and Michael

and to the memory of
Thomas

INTRODUCTION

This is the true story of a crisis in our family. Actually, there were two crises—Thomas' birth and Thomas' death. Thomas had Down Syndrome complicated by heart disease. His birth touched off a very real, very painful grief process over the loss of the expected child. Grief is not bad. It is necessary—necessary to begin a transformation process in which we construct a new identity. In this case, we were challenged to create an identity which included being the parents of a child with a developmental disability. We began to learn the meaning of patience. We also knew frustration. In fury, we learned to love.

When Thomas died at the age of seven months, he died a baby—a very lovable, cuddly baby. The crisis of his death stripped away our coping skills. It forced us to begin the hard work of adaptation anew. In a heartbeat, we had become a

1

bereaved family. Once again, our emotions took roller-coaster rides. Over time, healing became evident as I charted the journey through grief in a lovely cloth-covered journal given to me by a dear friend, Toni Dolan. In suffering, we began to see our strength. We learned to rejoice in the infinite beauty of Nature and the cyclical patterns which usher in rebirth. In the aftermath of intense grief, new values emerged. No, I would never have chosen this way, but I want to survive. Desire to survive is the necessary ingredient for healing to begin.

I believe we can create meaning, meaning which is rich and holistic, if we so choose. The message is:

EVEN IN THE WORST OF CIRCUMSTANCES, WE HAVE SOME CHOICES!

The choices are difficult. They do not come by chance. Before choices even become evident, we must endure many lonely hours of pain and hurt. The message here is not to pile on additional "shoulds" and "oughts." This story is shared to give hope. It is shared to give permission to grieve. It is also the culmination of a personal goal—to create meaning in Thomas' life just as it was. It is a love story. It is a story about learning to forgive life and moving on.

What is grief?
I thought I knew,
yet I know not its essence.

Peace of mind
    GONE.
Restful sleep
    GONE.
After nearly a year
of this thing called grief,
I realize I know not its essence.

Where is the other side of grief?
Tonight at 2 a.m., I wonder,
will I get to the other side?
    EVER?
I know not.
I know not.

But, wait . . .
a few minutes of writing
        of creating
        of pondering
usher in a brief respite.
A new awareness is forming.

Ups and downs
    Twists and turns
        Tears and love.

Can it be?
Grief is growth, too?
One pays a price.

The growth is NEVER
worth the price.

All is not lost.
We can go on.
There is much left
in spite of the
Ups and downs
    Twists and turns
        Tears and love.

I will survive
in spite of grief.
But please, let me be.
Understand that I need grief
    to ponder
    to reconstruct a new identity
    to get the sad out.

Grief is
Ups and downs
    Twists and turns
        Tears and love.

2/15/86

1

A CHILD IS BORN

I'll always remember October 13, 1984. It was a deceptively beautiful day—clear, sunny, warm. As a family, we were in the final days of awaiting our second child. Michael, ten days shy of four years, was very excited about becoming a "big brother." We had prepared him well, we thought, for what was to come. I had read countless books to him about having babies and educated him on the needs of babies using dolls and puppets. I felt so clever, so prepared. Little did I know how our lives would change in only two hours.

About 9 a.m. on that lovely Saturday, I awoke. Dave, my husband, had left earlier to go to his office to work on his dissertation. He was completing requirements for his Ph.D. in mechanical engineering from the University of Virginia. Michael and I planned on a casual day at home, I relishing the final days of being the mother of one. While preparing oatmeal for Michael, I began feeling some pains. Still, I was not positive this was IT, because I'd experienced three weeks of recurring false labor. I was so happy, so excited that we would now have two healthy children to grow up together. We had one healthy child. At least on a conscious level, there was no doubt in my mind that we would now have another. Just minutes later, with increased pressure and show, there was no question that it was time to sound the alarms.

Excited and full of confidence, I called Dave, telling him the time we had been waiting for had finally arrived. As planned, I phoned my mother, who was "on call" to stay with Michael. Labor came on quickly. By the time Dave arrived (9:40 a.m.), I was having the unmistakable urge to push. I'd always heard second labors were generally faster, but this was incredible. I could barely walk, but managed to lie down in the back of our station wagon. Dave got Michael into the car, since there wasn't time to wait until my mother arrived. Conveniently, we met her as we drove up our street, so Michael was transferred into her loving care. She was visibly excited about becoming a grandmother the second time around.

In response to the orders shouted from his laboring wife, Dave sped up the residential streets leading to the hospital, blowing the horn and passing cars all the way. We must have appeared quite comical. When we arrived at Virginia Baptist Hospital (10:00 a.m.), I could not walk another step, so the guard and Dave helped me on to a gurney. Normally, I am quite modest; but the act of childbirth has a way of removing all social propriety. As I was wheeled into the labor room, I remember asking if my obstetrician was on the premises, to which the answer was "yes." The nurse checked me, and I was immediately taken to delivery. No prepping, no anesthesia, which I did not want but might have taken out of fear had there been time. My obstetrician appeared and within the hour (11:12 a.m.), our second son, Thomas David, was born.

His entrance into the world seemed quick and uncomplicated. Thomas weighed 7 lb. 10 oz. His Apgar scores, an assessment of a newborn's health and vigor at one and five minutes after birth, were 9/9. Ten/ten represents a perfect score. I noticed that Thomas was quiet and less active than Michael had been at birth. I was not concerned—*individual differences only*, I reasoned, recalling T. Berry Brazelton's book, *Infants and Mothers—Differences in Development* (1). Dave and I held Thomas, then I was wheeled back to a labor room to recover and be checked. It seemed so easy the second time around. Having two wonderful boys was going to be great. Our family was complete. We had it all. Little did I know that this was the calm before the storm.

Dave then went to the car to get my suitcase. While he was gone, the obstetrician came in and somberly said, "We need to talk." "About what?" I gasped. Immediately, horror and panic rose in my chest. His next words I still cannot believe: "Your baby looks a little funny." Alone, I died a little inside. My breath was utterly taken away. *No! Not us! We have everything now. Dave, please hurry back.* "He has some signs, but I'm not sure," the doctor was saying. "We've called the pediatrician to come in and look at him. He'll come in and talk to you." In walked Dave and the horrible scenario was repeated. *Please, no! What the hell is happening here?*

I had taken excellent care of myself. No smoking or drinking. Nutritious foods. A total weight gain of 23 pounds. I CANNOT survive! The peaceful bliss of a lifetime turned to agonizing hell in a heartbeat. I had known what to do THIS time. Michael had grown and developed so beautifully. Maybe everything will be OK. Of course, this can't happen to us. There must be a mistake.

An eternity later, 30 minutes, the pediatrician came in and very tactfully and gently gave us his opinion. "Your baby has some of the characteristics associated with Down Syndrome." Here it is—the LABEL. *Oh, I want to die.* Are you sure? "He has only some of the characteristics. Chromosome tests must be done to make an absolute diagnosis." Much of the conversation is a blur. Dave gently held my hand. I felt totally numb. I couldn't even cry. We weren't in control after all. The tests had to be sent to the University of Virginia Medical Center, and it usually took two weeks to get the results. How could we survive that long? What should we say or do? How could we ever smile again?

After the pediatrician had left, we began trying to sort out the shattered pieces of our lives. I felt totally defeated. Caring for a handicapped child was definitely not in my plan. I was bitter and angry at all the people around me who were celebrating the joyous births of their healthy babies. I remembered how wonderful it had been when Michael was born. There were happy phone calls, visitors, flowers, cards. Whether right or wrong, we chose to "lie low" for a while. I had come to the hospital with a list of 20 names of people I wanted to call with the good news. The list never left my suitcase. The reality was overwhelming. I wanted to be relieved of this "burden." I did not see a baby. I saw only Down Syndrome. Robbed. Cheated forever. I did not see how life could ever be good again.

Looking back now, I know we pushed the doctors for answers. We heard clinical descriptions such as chromosome abnormality, mentally retarded, IQ 25-50, difficulty with reading and writing, usually able to perform self-help skills, and so on. I found myself reeling in terror. Our education didn't do us a bit of good in this situation. I'm sure that if we hadn't thought in terms of long-range implications, we would have had a somewhat easier adjustment. I saw my reading and study in psychology, parenting, and counseling reduced to complete insignificance. I felt helpless; I could not and did not want to meet the needs of a special child.

So many times during that first week, I wished to draw my last breath. My love for Dave and Michael kept me going. They provided the impetus for strength to endure what was, to me, the impossible. At this point, I felt no love for the "intruder" who had invaded my peaceful, predictable world. In my deep sorrow, I remember telling Dave that Michael was my "masterpiece." That was when I myopically thought that, as a mother, I totally could control the outcome—a beautiful, healthy, well-behaved child. What an order! Thomas was not the healthy little girl I had created in my mind who would grow long, brown hair which I would braid as my mother had done mine. Weeks before, I had gushingly bought a pretty doll in a department store for the daughter I was sure to have. Our society promotes this type of thinking. We think we have conquered all the mysteries of life. We want every-one to blend in, to fit neatly. The impact of the handicapped child brutally forces us to rewrite our scripts. Survival depends upon our ability to adapt.

When the obstetrician entered my room the next morning, I was crying. I had waked up crying. Maybe I never went to sleep. He took one look at me and said, "I'll send a social worker to see you." Translation: I can't talk to this hysterical woman. I wondered how he would feel if he had been in my place. I felt stripped and robbed of my identity as a competent, successful person. I was damned angry.

Why do we have such trouble allowing other people to express their feelings? These feelings need to be validated. Then, and only then, can we let go of our dreams and work with what we have. The period after birth is difficult. As women, we are fatigued. Our hormones are in flux. Add to that the reality of a baby with an incurable condition and the stress is unsurpassed. Dave accepted Thomas far more quickly than I; he said, "We can do it together." I did not think so.

10

Several of the nurses were very caring and warm to us. I'm sure they went home exhausted after listening to me. I know now that grief is selfish, and we need permission to be totally honest about how we are feeling. Unfortunately, I had had little contact with people with mental retardation, and my childhood memories were not kind. I recalled being grabbed and frightened as a child by an older child with Down Syndrome. In the 1950s, attitudes toward persons with special needs were shrouded in fear and misinformation, which I am sure added to my difficulty.

A number of people helped me survive the hospital stay. Susan, the social worker; Deborah, the mother of a four-year-old daughter with Down Syndrome; and Jean, the development instructor from Project Daniel. Project Daniel is the early intervention program in Lynchburg. It proved to be a lifeline for me, providing support and information. Each of these women gave me the marvelous gift of permission—permission to grieve bitterly. They patiently listened. They did not attempt to argue or reason with me. I would not have heard them anyway. Mostly, I cried. I did not call my friends. When I looked in the nursery window, I broke down crying. Other people were so happy. They had healthy, normal babies.

I now know the meaning of existential loneliness; there was no one who could take away my pain and rage. I kept badgering myself—Why had I wanted to have another baby anyway? Why hadn't I stopped while things were going well? Thomas was quiet and disinterested in nursing. I remember

11

telling Dave that we should take some pictures, because maybe we would find out he didn't have Down Syndrome after all. Down Syndrome seemed to take over my life. Over and over, I asked myself, "Why? Why us?"

After three everlasting days in the hospital, we went home. We insulated ourselves and let the answering machine record the calls. I didn't want to see anyone. We just wanted to pull together as a family and try to bring some order to our lives. Michael helped us emotionally. He was so excited. He was a big brother at last. He saw a baby. We actually were doing fairly well. Then, on Sunday morning, THE CALL came. By this time, we were convinced the test would be negative.

But, it wasn't. The test confirmed Down Syndrome. A scream stifled in my throat. Tears again. It's finally happened, that BIGGIE that irrevocably alters life forever. Frantically, I began to seek information. A strong believer in bibliotherapy, I ordered newsletters and a videotape about children with Down Syndrome. I found out the hard way to read only current material. Anything written prior to 1980 was too threatening, with terminology like "mongoloid," "defective," "moron," and so on. To some, these words may have little impact, but when they refer to your baby, they have the impact of lethal weapons. I found two excellent resources: *Time to Begin* (2) and *Helping Your Exceptional Baby* (3). These books became the most important books in my life. The terminology in them was non-threatening, and they described month-by-month stimulation activities and exercises to do with the special baby. Philosophically, they were the most positive resources I found.

Little by little, my grief began to lessen. But grief is a process that cannot be rushed or forced. It did no good whatsoever for people to tell me how I should feel or even attempt to answer why this happened to our child. People who said it was "God's will" made my anger resurface. Why must we attempt to answer the unanswerable? Why don't we just listen? Time, support, and being around Dave, Michael, and Thomas were the things that helped. We stuck together, and I feel very fortunate that we had each other's love.

When Thomas was a week and a half old, I called John David Smith, a former professor of mine from Lynchburg College. It goes without saying that I broke down crying on the phone. One year earlier, I had sat in his Survey of Exceptional Children class. I still consider it ironic that I chose this particular class as an elective toward my master's degree in counseling. I had thought that I appreciated exceptionalities. How different it was to be on the receiving end of the label. More than anything, we appreciated David's sensitivity and genuine love for exceptional children. He visited us at home. He was a supportive listener and filled in the gaps of our knowledge. But we still hurt. He asked us if Thomas had heart disease, which is prevalent in children with Down Syndrome. We said no, because an X-ray had been taken in the hospital and was normal. Once again, how naive we were. How much we would experience over the next six months.

Little by little, we began to tell our friends and relatives about Thomas' condition. My parents loved and accepted Thomas right away. Dave's mother in Indiana supported us and made plans to come to visit us before Thomas was even two months old. She, too, voiced her love and support of all of us. By this time, I was generally able to talk to people without breaking down into tears. I carried Thomas to the Mother's Support Group I had been co-leading at the Woman's Resource Center with my good friend Toni. Everyone "oohed" over Thomas. He did look precious in his little yellow crocheted outfit. Then, I broke the news to all of them at once. Everyone, I think, was in a state of shock. Some cried with me. Immediately, I became a "client" desperate for services, not the "facilitator" of support. The future seemed unbearably uncertain. I was frightened about the ramifications of parenting a child with special needs.

But, he did look precious in his little yellow crocheted outfit . . . .

DOWN SYNDROME

As I lay recovering from delivery . . .
blissful and peaceful,
certain that the second time would be much easier,
little did I know that my world was about to be shattered.

"We suspect Down Syndrome." they said.
The clocks stopped.
My heart raced.
My throat went dry . . .
then came the rage.

The worst was happening.
My life spun before me out of control.
My voice was trapped inside me.

All around me, people were jubilant over the births of
. . . healthy babies. I was alone.
What a cruel, unsafe place the hospital had become.
I wanted to flee . . . tell me it's not true.

The future no longer seemed exciting.
I did not give birth to a baby.
I gave birth to a label.

5/19/86

2

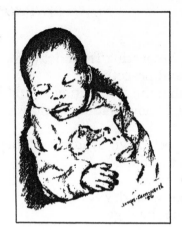

THOMAS - MY MISSION

The day I took Thomas to my support group was a turning point. On that day I felt accepted and strengthened by my peer group. One of my worst fears was that of rejection, that we would never be able to go on with our lives as before. But, as more and more people learned of Thomas' special needs, our lives began to change in significant ways. Personally, I began to realize that each human being has strengths and weaknesses, myself included. Beyond that was the realization that we can be acceptable just as we are. As I listened to "Mr. Rogers" with my children, I found new meaning in the words, "You are special, there's not another one like you in the whole world"(4). It was as if having Thomas gave me permission to accept my own and others' limitations.

I began meeting new people through the Association for Retarded Citizens meetings—people who generated love and who were not hung up on labels. Many, many people reached out with kindness to our family with cards, calls, and information. In essence, I found a new support group in which I felt comfortable to express myself, both positively and negatively. As I listened to other families who were coping and adapting to their special children's needs, I began to feel "so can we."

There are those few whom I knew well who have never acknowledged Thomas' birth or death. At first, this silence was very painful. Now I can accept their discomfort and not dwell on it. We have really appreciated those who did make the effort to show us they cared. It takes a lot of courage to look at the dark, scary side of life. Most of us don't do it by choice.

Tina, from Project Daniel, became very significant in our lives. Each week, she came to our home bringing ideas to stimulate Thomas, as well as compassion and gentle love. She pointed out the lovely things she saw in Thomas but never pushed me to love more than I was ready. Many cold, wintry mornings, she was the highlight of my day. I waited for her car to pull up; as soon as it did, I felt that I could make it another day. She reduced my isolation and was sensitive to Michael's need for attention, as well. Some days she brought something for Michael to play with, too. Often, we would just talk, usually with me bursting with words and she patiently listening and supporting. When unaware people in stores commented about Thomas' small size or used such terms as "mongoloid," I would be set into a tailspin and couldn't wait to tell her about it. I was very needy.

I now realize that most people do not intend to be cruel. They simply do not realize how hard it is to hear your child referred to this way. This grief is real; it is powerful. At this point, people need good listeners, not moralizers or lecturers. Hearing "shoulds" and "oughts" only blocks the grieving process and increases the physical and mental burden of grieving. It is very important that people be allowed to grieve over their losses, whatever they are.

After a while, the pain was greatly reduced, and I was able to go on with the process of living and maximizing Thomas' potential. Another wise person, our pediatrician, told me not to rush the bonding with Thomas, that it would come gradually. He was so right. Another thing that he did that helped was to compliment me on my work and efforts with both boys.

I plunged into my new role reading every good resource I could find. I drew Dick Bruna pictures in brilliant colors and hung them all around Thomas's bassinet to encourage head lifting. Bruna's books are simple, colorful picture books which are interesting to babies. I checked them out from the library and drew the animal and people designs with colorful magic markers. Thomas lifted his head for long periods of time to "study" each design carefully. I was captivated by his interest in the pictures. He was rewarding my efforts.

I played different types of music on the piano and tape deck and read to both boys at the same time. Michael provided a beautiful language model to Thomas. We encouraged him to talk and sing to his baby brother. The bonding that developed between our two boys was so satisfying to see. They communicated in a language all their own. I used a penlight in a darkened room to stimulate Thomas' tracking skills. Watching his eyes follow the light up and down, to the left and right, and in a circular motion was thrilling to me. Although he was only a month old, he was learning. As mother and child, we began to connect.

In short, the bonding did develop. Thomas became a challenge to me, and every response began to surprise and delight me and to further ignite my attempts to help him. Yet, there were still those dark days when I backslid. I found myself trying to see into the future or longing for the simpler past. What I realize now is that we, parents of special children, need to slow down and take it one day at a time. I began to realize that the enigmatic "future" was not going to slap me in the face all at once. I began to see the child first, the handicap second.

I took Thomas to the pediatrician every two weeks because he was not gaining weight very well. I fed and fed him, yet the scales did not reflect my efforts. At six weeks, he was still close to his birth weight. I was beside myself, because I had nursed successfully before. I was beginning to feel like a failure. I emphatically told the doctor that something must be wrong. The first month I could understand why he did not gain, but not now. The pediatrician was supportive and sensitive and ordered an EKG and another chest X-ray.

Again, we had a major surprise. The X-ray revealed a cardiac malformation. Thomas was immediately put on digoxin and lasix to make his heart work more efficiently and to remove excess fluids. Within three days, we were at the University of Virginia Medical Center to see the pediatric cardiologist. A more extensive test was done—the echocardiogram. Thomas had a serious cardiac malformation—the complete AV Canal Defect and Patent Ductus Arteriosis. Essentially, there were two holes in his heart causing increased blood flow. This inefficiency led to his lack of energy and failure to gain weight. Surgery was needed in his first year of life, but he needed to gain weight first. *Catch 22.* The heart medications and almost constant feedings did help him gain the needed weight. I began feeding him high calorie foods and extra formula after breastfeedings.

Christmas came and went. Surgery seemed an eternity away. Yet, I had a mission: help Thomas gain weight to increase his chances of successful surgery, while continuing to stimulate his senses. This was a full-time job. Fortunately, Dave helped in every way—transporting Michael to and from nursery school, grocery shopping, laundry, and so on. Thomas was tracking objects very well by this time.

Michael was a help, too, in diapering and talking to Thomas. We told him that Thomas needed extra help to grow and learn, and Michael respected this need. He seemed secure enough about his position in the family that he didn't feel threatened. I checked out books from the library to read to Michael about the hospital and surgery. We tried to answer his questions and make him a part of things; yet there were days I was stressed to the limit and fractious. But we worked together as a family. Thomas ceased to be an "it"; he was now "Thomas David" with full rank and privilege in our family; we would be there for him, as we would for Michael.

Thomas was gentle and lovable, rarely fretful. Like other babies, he began to smile, giggle, grasp, and bat. He developed a delightful personality. I began to think about how many things we take for granted in this life—walking, talking, reading, writing, other people. Yet, at times, I still grieved over the seemingly more certain future of a child without special needs. But, because I knew all along that Thomas was "at risk," I did not take his achievements for granted. Some days I would just gaze at him in amazement. Oh yes, my love did grow.

I continued to read with a vengeance. Gross motor skills were beginning to lag, but I knew that Thomas' heart disease was at the root of that. So I focused on the areas that were appropriate for Thomas. Step by step, he showed me that he was a beautiful, gentle little boy who could grow and develop. People seemed to love him; for better or worse, people constantly commented that he didn't "look different" and was "so alert." I think many people, not just the Farnsworth family, have grown from knowing Thomas.

We were again rather stable in our day-to-day routines when, in February, Thomas began to sound congested. Because of his heart problems, he was more at risk. He developed pneumonia and was hospitalized in Virginia Baptist for eleven days. I stayed in the room with him almost constantly; but Dave, my mother, and my sister relieved me so I could spend some time with Michael. When one child is hospitalized and another is at home, parenting is very difficult. I felt pulled in both directions, wanting to be with both boys. Logistically, this desire was impossible. I kept in touch with Michael by telephone and mail, and when I did get to be with him, I tried to make it quality time.

Tina was there through the good and bad. She visited us in the hospital bearing gifts, magazines, and fruit. Thomas pulled through the pneumonia, and we came home. I imagined this illness would set him back, but I was wrong. The month of March was a wonder to behold. He grew stronger, more sociable, and began kicking his legs and waving his arms more than ever before. He was charming. I believed in Thomas more than ever.

I had no doubts that the surgery would give him more strength and allow him to gain more weight. Day by day, we were making it. Some days, I felt very low, but watching Thomas was very rewarding. I was up two or three times in the night to feed him, but I did not resent it because I knew he needed those extra feedings to improve his chances in surgery.

We were ready and optimistic for the next step—surgery. Never did we believe we would leave the hospital without Thomas.

Why? Why? Why us?
I've asked myself a thousand . . .
        no, a million times.
Our lives were perfect.
We were so very happy.
We were where we wanted to be.
A second son was like "icing on the cake."

After struggling and fighting life,
I think I know "why."
It's the "why" that only we could create.
Look at what we have to offer.
We are dedicated. We have love.
We know joy. We have a lot to give.
Dave was right, "We can do it together."

The answer was there all along
. . . as answers often are . . .
waiting to be discovered
. . . inside.

4/9/86

3

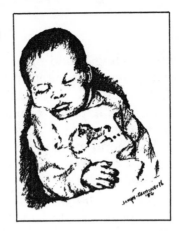

OUR HOSPITAL HOME

On April 8, 1985, our family was excited, hopeful that Thomas would find the help he needed at the University of Virginia Medical Center. He was active and sociable that crisp, sunny morning. He looked precious in his yellow suit with a locomotive applique on the front. Michael was excited and proud that he was included in helping us prepare and accompanying us to Charlottesville. I'd talked with a number of people whose children had had open heart surgery or knew of others who had. The information was both positive and helpful. We had waited what seemed like years for this day—we were ready.

Thomas now weighed 13 lb. 8 oz., not bad at all considering the severity of his heart disease. I remember feeling proud of him and proud of us that we'd gotten the weight on him.

UVA hospital is a world away from the smaller Virginia Baptist Hospital in our town. As a teaching hospital, UVA is larger, older, and full of activity. We found more people in and out of our space because of the seemingly endless medications and procedures that were needed. I say "space" because there are no private rooms, as in Virginia Baptist Hospital. Parents can stay with their child and attempt sleep on a chair that reclines. After three nights of constant interruption and tension, I was exhausted. The staff members were very qualified and caring; fatigue is just part of hospital life. The experience, though difficult, taught me some very important lessons about life, its unfairness, its transience, its beauty in spite of pain.

On South 2, the pediatric floor, the nurses became extended family. I'll never forget Marilu and Michele, who were extremely supportive and helpful to me. It seemed that they went the extra mile for us. They complimented us on the stimulating environment we had set up for Thomas in his crib—colorful things to see, classical music to hear, and lots of touching. These women invited me to lunch when they detected my stress and strain, a nice change of pace.

Our admittance was on Monday with numerous baseline tests and history taking. On Tuesday, Thomas was taken down to the cardiac catheterization lab. Cardiac catheterization is a diagnostic procedure to determine the structural and functional nature of the heart. In this procedure, dye is injected and pictures are taken so the surgical strategy can be planned by the medical team. Time spent waiting for a child to be brought back to the room from any procedure seemed endless. I was always anxious and frightened that something might go wrong. When Thomas was brought back up, I cried tears of relief. He was very sleepy the rest of the day. These were long, lonely hours, and any card, note, or call from home was an unexpected delight. I feel that such gestures are the stuff from which courage is made.

On Wednesday, the cardiologists and surgeons spoke with us. The catheterization showed that the pulmonary artery pressures were extremely high and that the lungs had already begun to show permanent changes. Most definitely, surgery was indicated as soon as possible. The two heart defects—Complete AV Canal Defect and Patent Ductus Arteriosis—would be repaired in surgery.

On Thursday, April 11, I carried Thomas down to the operating room around 6 a.m. These moments were so sweet and special. I kissed him and placed him in the arms of the anesthesiologist. As I did, Thomas gently opened his eyes as if to say "bye, mommy." I began to weep, thinking that that could be the last time I would see him alive. It was an overwhelming experience. I could not get the image of the surgeon's scalpel out of my mind. I ached in sympathy for the little patient.

I then went back to the South 2 room, collected all of our things, and carried them to our van. Thomas would not return to that room. I remember the intense feeling of numbness, as I got into the van and drove to Hearthstone House, where I would stay at night until Thomas was out of ICU. I checked in and broke down crying to Dan, the Director of Hearthstone. The house is modeled after the Ronald McDonald Houses and is sponsored by churches, civic groups, and individual contributions. It became my "home away from home." And what a refuge it turned out to be. It was here that I truly realized that I was not alone. In fact, our family had it easy compared to some. For the first time in months, I felt a part of the majority. Human diversity was the rule, not the exception.

Here I met other parents who were also frightened about the future of their children. I'll never forget Angie, age 7, bald from chemotherapy, who had had countless surgeries and who cried with pain at night. There was also Joshua, a toddler, who had an inoperable brain tumor. He was blind and undergoing six weeks of radiation therapy. He was predicted to have only one more year to live. There was Lynn, age 2, who had an operation to create an esophagus with part of her intestine. There was Ann who was severely facially deformed from the cord wrapping around her head in utero. She was classified as profoundly mentally retarded, and the plastic surgeons her foster mother consulted said there was nothing they could do to help her. Her birth parents chose never to take her home from the hospital. So much pain was concentrated in those walls. We shared our lives, our anger, our setbacks, our victories.

In all my life, I'd never been aware of so much hurt and suffering. Some are able to make the adaptations. Some are not. Some exemplify tremendous courage. I will never forget Darlene, age 19, who worked at Hearthstone. Because of cancer, she had had her left leg amputated at age 14. She is adept at everything—driving, swimming, and stair climbing. Never once did I hear her complain. She led a full and active life and was engaged and attending college when I met her. Her zest for life was a model for us all. These were only some of the wonderful people I met at Hearthstone. I will carry them with me always.

Dave drove to Charlottesville on the morning of the surgery. He had been carrying the load at home with chores, spending time with Michael, and working as much as possible. We were lucky to have a wonderful nursery school experience for Michael, a number of supportive friends and my parents and sister who cared for Michael some of the time. We had been told that we would hear how Thomas was by noon on Thursday. Dave arrived at the hospital at about 11 a.m., and we went into the lounge for surgical patients' families to wait for the news. Both of us found the waiting almost unbearable.

It was 3 p.m. before one of the surgeons came out to speak with us. With the three extra hours, we were expecting the worst. When our name was called, we could barely walk to the conference room. The surgeon looked exhausted. He seemed to care so much for "his babies." It seemed an eternity before he said that Thomas had made it through the surgery but definitely could not be considered "out of the woods." The repairs had been made, but the pulmonary artery pressures were still elevated.

Thomas would now remain in the surgical intensive care unit (SICU) where everything imaginable was monitored round the clock. We could visit for limited periods four times a day. There was a private 24-hour nursing staff, and we were given a direct telephone number that we could call, day or night, to ask about him. Many nights I slept a few hours and woke up in a state of alarm. I made numerous calls to check on Thomas—so did Dave from home. I always hung up feeling some temporary relief.

I was not prepared to see Thomas the first time after the operation. If you have never seen a person following open heart surgery, there can be no preparation. When it is your child, your first reaction is, "My God, what have I permitted to happen to my son!" Bandages covered his entire chest area. There were many wires, tubes, and monitors attached to every crack and crevice of his tiny body. I nearly fainted from the overwhelming reality of what he had been through. Staff personnel were standing on each side of us and behind us. They were prepared should one of us faint. I felt grateful to the surgeons for their dedication and the stress they must have felt during this lengthy, difficult operation. After a few minutes, we regained our composure and once again felt some degree of optimism.

When Dave returned to Lynchburg after a few days and Thomas was stable, I found myself in Charlottesville with time on my hands. I took the opportunity to "recharge" my battery before full-time care resumed. Thomas Jefferson's University is so beautiful in the springtime with the tulips, azaleas, and dogwood in bloom. I felt a tinge of sadness that we would not be home to enjoy the beautiful colors, but the grounds more than made up for the absence. Early in the morning after visiting my son in the SICU, I strolled the grounds, allowing my senses to take in its beauty. I explored the massive stacks in the library and took the opportunity to research Down Syndrome further. It was here that I learned never to open books about Down Syndrome written prior to 1980. I found the negative terminology ("moron," etc.) extremely offensive, and the prognoses horrifying. I did find one recently written book, *Cara* (5), to be an excellent resource. I sat on the lawn early in the morning studying its pages. Thomas had planted seeds of change, which I did not fully understand or accept. I had no way of knowing then what an impact he would have on my life.

In addition, I went shopping, often sending Michael a card, or purchasing a small item just to "keep in touch" between our visits. A number of times, he and Dave drove up together; I spent time exploring or lunching with Michael, while Dave visited Thomas. I missed Michael so much; yet, when you have no choice, you adapt as well as possible. People may wonder how a mother could actually have fun when her child is recovering from major surgery. Again, the answer is, you adapt. You come to realize that your child is under the best care possible and that you cannot function without respite.

31

During all this time, I continued to pump breast milk. I felt this was a gift of love that I could provide to help Thomas. Also during this time, I occasionally lay on my bed at Hearthstone House wondering how all this could possibly have happened to our family. I cried some. Some days on the street, I would see a pregnant woman looking so happy or a mother loving her baby, and I would walk away with tears streaming down my face. Sometimes, I would say aloud, "I hate you, God!" (It is okay, I believe, because God is big enough to take all our anger.) These were extreme circumstances. I had a right to be angry, for a time.

Also during this time, I had many friendly people to talk to: nurses, doctors, other "waiting" parents. Some of these people I miss even today. I came to see physicians as human beings, apart from the role, who were not all-knowing gods, but people like you and me. This was an important discovery for me. I began to understand the responsibility of the patient or the patient's advocate to take an active role in health care.

After Thomas had been in the SICU about a week and a half, he graduated to the Pediatric Intensive Care Unit (PICU). Here, I was able to spend more time with him, and the staff and I became quite comfortable with one another. Once again, I brought out the mobiles, pictures, and music. Thomas was more alert now, and I was able to begin nursing him again. I was amazed that modern medicine could open the heart of an infant, repair the problem, and the child would still be able to function.

By now, death did not cross my mind. We thought we were homeward bound. I'd become quite familiar with the monitors and treatments Thomas was being given. This knowledge helped me stay actively involved and enabled me to communicate with new staff members. Once again, Thomas was smiling and lovable. I felt as though we had scaled Mt. Everest.

After another week and a half, Thomas graduated to the pediatric floor, South 2, the last step, we thought, before leaving for home. The nurses welcomed us back to their charge. After a few days, another cardiac catheterization was scheduled to assess the pulmonary artery pressures. Bad news! The pressures had not gone down, as expected. The next day Thomas did not feed as well. He spiked a fever, but we did not expect this to be critical. On Saturday, I drove to Lynchburg to spend a night with Michael. Dave stayed at Hearthstone in case one of us was needed. At 6 a.m. Sunday, he received a call from the cardiologist, informing him that Thomas was critically ill and being moved back to the PICU. Dave called me at home at 8 a.m. and told me to return immediately.

Hence began the last ten days of Thomas David's short life. Much of this time seems a blur now, yet episodes are vividly etched in my mind. Some days I felt so competent. Other days exhaustion set in, and I felt heavily burdened. Dave and I never felt that Thomas was going to die. I continued to work on a needlepoint project for his room as I sat by his crib. Waiting. Wondering. We stayed actively involved in his care and aware of changes in medications and treatments. I believe our involvement helped us cope with the roller-coaster ride of the last days.

Then, on Monday and Tuesday, May 6 and 7, Thomas had a number of episodes of heart arrhythmia, falling blood pressure, kidney failure, swelling, blueness, and lung collapse. These days were a living nightmare and left Dave and me emotionally wrenched. We cried. We ached.

We were told that Thomas was "spiralling down" and probably would not live through the night. These were horrible scenes, almost unreal with suctioning that left the staff exhausted. Hands shook as new meds were rushed into the IV line. I felt as though I was caving in. Never had I experienced such fatigue. We hung on. We stayed the night near his bed. We wanted to be there if . . . . The night lasted an eternity. Night became day, and the little guy stabilized. We believed he was going to do it, even though the doctors gave us no reason to hope. Yet, they respected our need to have hope. Even then, I still went into the women's room and secretly expressed breast milk. I was determined to give this gift to Thomas if. . . .

The steady beep, beep, beep
of the heart monitor
becomes commonplace . . .
it tells us that our son
is still alive.

The awesome technology
of the ICU becomes . . .
almost soothing.
The staff knows us,
we know them . . .
sometimes we even joke,
share stories,
exchange food,
hug
. . . and wait.

Then the screen goes wild,
people begin to scramble,
hands shake . . . theirs and ours,
pulses race . . . theirs and ours,
heroics are attempted . . .
suctioning that leaves nurses
exhausted and pale.
They care so much.
They love that baby, too.

We wonder, "Will the end be THIS way?"
Days and nights run together.
Exhaustion takes over.

Then, equilibrium is restored.
People take breaks.
There are tears . . . and hugs.

Dave and I share hopes and dreams . . . we grow.
We do not wish to grow any more.
It is not for us to decide.
The end . . . or the beginning?

And then,
   we wait,
      we wonder.

But we never
   lose hope.

No one is ever prepared
   to lose
      a child.

          2/23/86

4

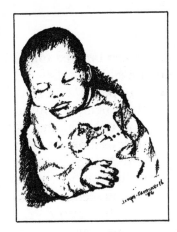

OUR SON DIED

On Thursday Thomas remained stable. Dave and I were a little smug, thinking that he would be the miracle case after all. Dave asked me if I would feel comfortable if he returned home to check on Michael, do some errands, and submit a report at work. Since Thomas seemed so much better, we both felt o.k. about Dave's leaving the hospital. He said that he would return by 8:00 that night. The day was uneventful with the routine medications, treatments, and evaluations by the staff.

At about 6:00 p.m., I told one of the nurses that Thomas looked a bit puffy and slightly blue. I began feeling anxious even though the monitors indicated no change and sounded no alarms. I wanted Dave to come back. Like clockwork, my husband walked into the unit at 8:00 p.m. Instantly, I breathed a sigh of relief.

At this point, I began thinking about how much we had been through over the last seven months, especially Thomas—the ups, the downs, the other serious illnesses we saw, the other parents crying in the halls, almost breaking down from stress. This, in itself, was an education for me. The BIGGIES always seemed to happen to someone else, someone I didn't know very well. Until now. I believe a power bigger than we are sustains us through such tragedies. The love and concern of other people is so important and so powerful. To me, God is in these people; their concern builds a bridge toward survival and recovery. I have learned from this crisis to break down, show my vulnerability, and to ask for help. As a controlled sort of person, this was an unwelcome role for me, but one which has enriched my life a thousandfold. I have learned to accept help; in turn, I can now genuinely give help.

In the depths of my heart, I began to see how very hard Thomas was trying to live. I believe he felt our presence and love. He fought and fought, yet I came to the realization that it was really quite selfish to want him to continue fighting and struggling. Then, I did something which may sound very strange and unbelievable. I let go. I let the way of life take over. I remember clearly how that felt and when I did it. I said, "O.K., my little angel, I know how hard this life has been. I understand. If you need to leave us now, go in peace and love. As your mother, I will never forget you, and I know that I am a better person for having had you just the way you are. I am becoming stronger." Although I felt pain, I also felt a wave of peace and resolution. We had come full circle. Hate and love. Love is . . . holding on . . . and letting go.

At about 10:00 p.m., I left the unit to make a telephone call. Dave stayed at Thomas' bedside. In a fifteen-minute span, his physical body began to shut down, not violently as in the previous episodes, but gently. Dave ran to the phone to get me. We raced back to Thomas. On one level, it was tragic to watch Thomas die; on another level, it was one of my life's peak experiences. I let go of my personal agenda. Thomas was in the driver's seat. He carried out a brilliant performance to the end. As I write these words sixteen months later, I feel the pain of the long absence, the longing to touch his soft baby skin. That night, I felt peace. It was as though Thomas led us step by step to acceptance of his death.

The young attending physician that night allowed us to see her beautiful, gentle tears. We all knew that every possible medical and respiratory measure had been taken. When the heart monitor was down to four beats per minute, we knew that we were witnessing actual physical death. Gently and lovingly, the nurses removed the tapes, wires, and tubes. They, too, blessed us with their tears. Dave and I picked Thomas' body up, sat very close together in an embrace, and held and rocked him *for the last time*. The nurses pulled the curtain around us and told us to stay as long as we wished. Dave and I reviewed the last almost seven months of life with Thomas—the good and the bad times.

39

Though tragic, I felt a sense of immense peace that comes from resolution. The days had been long and hard. We were tired of being separated, of eating hospital food, of living out of suitcases, of hearing frightened little children who do not understand what is happening to them. It is a terrible ordeal as a parent to be so out of control. It is so unfair that beautiful children are critically ill and, in fact, die.

We do not know the answer to the "whys" that haunt us. We struggle and rant and rave until we become aware that we are not the only ones who have suffered, until we begin to see that even in tragedy we have some choices. What possibly can we choose when we suffer, when we watch our children suffer, when part of us dies when they take that last breath? For a long, long time, it seems that God has forsaken us, indeed, that we have been punished. We embark on a process. Over time, we see our strength, our power to choose. Until that time, we must engage in the difficult work of grief.

The cardiologist, the PICU head physician, and several off-duty nurses appeared shortly after Thomas died. They had asked to be called if he died. I thought this was a beautiful gesture of caring. I was recalling the lovely work of Dr. Elisabeth Kübler-Ross which allowed me to see that these moments, too, were priceless. My reaction was no longer to fight death, but to accept it and greet it. This was my gift to Thomas, to simply enjoy him for the last time. Yes, those of us who are left behind have terrible pain, but we have also been enriched.

I don't presume to know what is on the other side of this life, yet I do not fear it. C. S. Lewis wrote, "The best is perhaps what we understand least"(6).

I recall leaving the hospital unit around midnight. Dave and I, both stunned, were surprised that the world was going on as before. There was life all around us, yet our son had just died. Nurses were talking, patients were coughing, sirens wailed outside, and cars and trucks sped along the avenue. Life continued to flow in the midst of personal crisis. Dave and I walked the street to the motel and staggered to our room. There, we cried and talked. I picked up an envelope and began to write. Suddenly, I knew I had to compose a brief eulogy for Thomas' funeral. We both shared thoughts and asked Michael for input the next day. This is what we wrote:

> *Even though Thomas David's life was short, it was rich with meaning. We have grown and continue to grow by having had him live with us. Gently, he loved us and asked nothing in return. He was a fighter. He endured more in his short life than most of us will ever face. We had truly hoped he would beat the odds.*

> *He taught us a greater meaning of love and life. He showed us how to appreciate the natural graces of life, like the flowers and being together as a family. We hoped for family walks together and to show him the ocean. He taught us that life is not fair, but it's how we respond to it that matters. We cherish his precious life and know that it was not in vain. He prepared us for his death and left us peacefully. We*

will miss him greatly, yet we find strength in know-
ing he is at peace. He was a true gift.
                    In love,
            Mommy, Daddy, and Michael

At about 4:00 a.m., we were finally exhausted and sleep came. We slept a few hours and awoke to begin the busy ordeal of making funeral arrangements and informing the world. When I woke up, I kept saying to myself, "My child died last night." The reality sank in gradually, not all at once. I felt very agitated and wanted to get home to be with Michael. My sister, Wanda, was at our house with him. I remember a feeling of disorientation. I wanted to be home, yet I wanted to go to the funeral home right away to settle all plans. I was totally indecisive. Agitated. Neither of us could bear the thought of food, but I did drink milk on the way back to Lynchburg.

In the car, I remember looking at Dave and thinking, "Why does he have to go through this? He is so kind and good. He doesn't deserve this." And Michael. He was such a loving big brother. Why, damnit? Since we passed Diuguid's Funeral Home on the way to our house, we decided to stop there first. The staff was so professional and caring. One by one, we planned the details of the funeral. I nearly fainted from shock when we went into the large room filled with caskets to select one for Thomas. Our son in a casket! Over and over, we faced new realities—realities we'd never thought about before. The facades of life were stripped away.

All day I kept thinking about Thomas' body coming home in the funeral home's station wagon. Obsessions such as this and reviewing scenes over and over are part of the work of grief. It is exhausting work, but necessary to process the loss. I felt like I was in a dream. At first, there was a protective numbness. Raw pain came later.

I called David Leonard, minister of First Unitarian Church of Lynchburg. We'd asked him to conduct Thomas' burial service. David had been a tremendous support over the months. He always seemed to capture our feelings accurately and to validate our experience. He modeled how to help a person in grief. How important it is to have a person or persons who can give this help when we most need it.

We decided to bury Thomas at 11:00 a.m. on Monday. We chose a simple graveside service, since the May weather was so beautiful. With those things settled came what hurt most—telling Michael. We longed to protect him from the pain, but we knew we could not.

We had talked and read little books on death to him long before, but it is much more difficult when you have your own pain, as well. We'd told him about his Grandpa Farnsworth, who died long before he was born. When we got home, we had him come outside into the yard with us. We began by saying, "You know how very sick Thomas has been." He'd visited Thomas in the hospital numerous times. "Well, darling, he died last night." At this point, we all embraced, sat in the yard, and cried together. I remember saying, "It is o.k. to cry and feel sad, because we'll all miss Thomas." Dave said, "Thomas doesn't feel any hurt or pain." We also told him that it was nobody's fault, that sometimes life just isn't fair. "Later, we will begin to remember the good times we had with Thomas."

It is also very important to tell a child that he cannot "catch" the illness and die himself. Never should death be compared to sleep. We felt more comfortable saying that we do not know exactly what happens after death, but we are certain that there is no pain. Numerous times over the months since Thomas' death, Michael has asked why the doctors could not fix Thomas' heart. We've always said that we know the doctors did everything they possibly could, but sometimes it just doesn't work. It is important to accept all feelings the child expresses and to continue to support him. (Some good books for children about death are listed in the resource list.)

On Friday afternoon, Mike Moore, an old friend who worked at Diuguid's, came to the house to pick up the little outfit Thomas would be buried in. It was a white, crocheted sweater set with tiny pastel flowers embroidered on it. There were a little bonnet and socks to match. Mike was reassuring and told us that it was important to answer siblings' questions as honestly as possible.

Later that afternoon, Dave, Michael, and I went to see Thomas at the funeral home. I will never forget this experience. Thomas was a beautiful sight to my weary eyes. All the puffiness, blueness, and discomfort was gone. He looked as if he had never been sick a day in his life. He looked so natural, even angelic. We all cried. Michael had brought Thomas' little toy dog and some pictures he drew and placed them gently in the casket. We reassured Michael that Thomas was not in any pain.

How difficult it is to see one of your babies crying over the body of your other baby. You would give anything to make it different, but you know that you cannot. You have to have the strength to let it happen and instill in the grieving child the courage to face the pain, feel it, and have the faith that life will go on and be worth living again. There will be sadness for a long time, but you learn to crawl, then walk through it. Children look to us to model how to respond to crises. If we show them that it is appropriate to be sad, to cry, to talk about our feelings, and then to reconstruct our lives and rediscover joy, they will most likely adapt to the loss in a positive way.

On Saturday the obituary appeared in the paper. Company started coming bearing food, gifts for Michael, and concern for all of us. We were astounded that so many people reached out. We received cards from people we barely knew. Such concern is powerful. People were sending the message that they cared about us. Sometimes this is all you have to go on. You become stronger.

Many people listened as we told our story over and over. Listening is so important, and it takes courage and patience to really listen to pain. Often people want to make it better quickly. This effort is not helpful. We all grieve in our own way, at our own pace. My former professor, David, came to the funeral home and listened patiently while I poured out the agony in my heart. What a help that was. Grief is necessary. We need many supportive listeners to move through the process.

Sunday was an especially searing Mother's Day. It seemed like a big slap to have my child lying in the funeral home on Mother's Day. For a long time, I was incensed that God could allow such an injustice. On Sunday night, it rained as if the heavens were bursting with grief. I felt we had been given a beautiful gift on Monday morning, the day of the funeral, when we awoke to a fresh, clean, sunny day. The birds' songs were so lovely. The flowers glistened in the sunlight. Mechanically, we bathed, dressed, and got into the car to drive to the cemetery. I wore a black dress accented in white, black symbolic of my grief, white symbolic of life and hope.

Many people came to the funeral and that meant so much to us. Nobody "likes" funerals, but it is a loving gesture of support. I appreciated each face I saw there that day. The funeral was designed according to our wishes, and we felt good about that. It was important to me to establish some sense of competency as soon as possible. The funeral was over. It was time to go home, to return to the business of living.

After all the turbulent
days and nights,
nights and days,
there was calm.
Thomas was peaceful.
We mistook the peace
as getting better, yet
we humans never know for sure.

We continued to massage him
... with gentle fingers,
to talk and sing in loving voices
and to say ...
    It is OK if you must leave us,
    but we'll take you and love you
    any way we can.

We were getting ready ...
but we knew not which way
the die would fall.

On Thursday,
Thomas was quiet and peaceful all day.
Surely, the doctors were wrong THIS TIME.
Then, in only a few moments, late that night,
the beautiful butterfly was freed.

Thomas made the transition ...
with the aplomb of a hero.
Gently and lovingly, the nurses wept ...
as they removed the tapes, wires, and tubes.
The attending physician allowed us to see
her beautiful, gentle tears.

We kissed him . . . and rocked him for hours
   FOR THE LAST TIME.
I believe he waited for us
. . . to be able to endure the blow.
Stunned, Dave and I walked through deserted corridors
. . . now still from the activity of the day.

So this is what it is like.
We left our hospital home.
We walked the street to the motel.
We were hot, then cold . . . dazed.
We were startled to hear
. . . horns blowing
. . . laughter from speeding cars
. . . sirens . . . another life in limbo?
We REALLY SAW traffic lights changing.
There was life all around us.
Who are we now?
Where do we go from here?

We both know . . . through words unspoken . . .
life will never be the same.
Our challenge is to learn from Thomas
. . . to be freer than ever before
   . . . to learn to be
      . . . butterflies while we live.

5/15/86

5

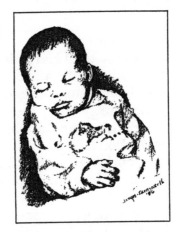

AFTER THE FUNERAL

After the funeral, the real grieving began. Friends returned to their own lives, as they should. The inspirational cards and wholesome food stopped coming. People went back to work. I woke up in the same house, but it was not the same. I was left to face the reality of the empty crib, the diaper service that must be canceled, the baby clothes that were no longer needed, the bills that must be paid, the grocery shopping, cooking, and laundry that had accumulated. I washed his little clothes and held them to my body and wept.

In spite of my pain, life went on. Routine activities, like writing checks, were difficult. I had to pay for the obituary in the local newspaper, the final diaper service delivery, the hospital bills, the druggist charges—this I had to do and I could barely remember my name. Balancing the checkbook was impossible; I could not concentrate that long.

Going into public places at first was like a roller-coaster ride. One day while Dave and I were sitting in McDonald's, alarms on the ovens went off. I bolted upright in my seat. The alarms sounded like those on the heart monitor when Thomas was in crisis.

I saw people, acquaintances, who asked, "Where's the baby?" How could they have known that he died? A couple of people looked into the back of my van and asked, "Where is the car seat?" I felt awkward. I had to say over and over, "He died." As I still must. It was necessary to process the loss. I'd gotten used to night feedings, extra formula, medications, diapers, and doctor visits. Part of me had died. There was a real void at first.

My emotions were unpredictable. One day while visiting someone in the hospital, I saw the guard who helped me onto the gurney the day Thomas was born. Seeing him brought up the sharp pain of that day. The unnatural hurt. The immediate halt to our dreams of the healthy, normal child. Another day while Michael was playing at the park, a little girl with Down Syndrome came running up and got on the merry-go-round with him. Seeing her unleashed a river of pent-up tears. She saw my pain and ran over to hug me. What a lovely smile she had.

Suddenly it seemed as if everyone I knew was pregnant or had just had a healthy baby. I cried over everything. On TV, all I saw were Pampers commercials or women in labor. It hurt so much. As one of my friends said, Thomas died "every day," not just one day. I felt that surely my heart would split in two. My sanity seemed threatened.

The March of Dimes campaign enraged me. The advertisements seemed to prescribe the formula for a healthy baby. Early prenatal care. Good nutrition. No smoking. No alcohol. Exercise. I did all that. What happened? Driving in the car, all I saw were mothers pushing strollers and buses for children with handicaps. Now I understood completely Elisabeth Kübler-Ross' words, "Dying is easy, but living is hard" (7). Never before had living been this hard.

People say the darnedest things to those of us who are grieving. Things like, "Now you can get on with your life." Another asked, "Are you glad he died?" How simplistic. How naive. All relationships are complex. All relationships have positive and negative components. I would always want my child to be healthy and "normal," but I had invested in the relationship with Thomas just as he was. I learned to see the baby first, the handicap second. I began to see that there are no guarantees in life. Mental retardation can happen to anyone. Accidents happen. People do die young.

Someone gave me a long novel to read. Halfway through it, a mother gave birth to a baby with Down Syndrome. The mother smothered the child. I wonder even today how reading that book possibly could have lifted my burden. It was devastating to read.

Others told me that it was God's will that Thomas was handicapped and that he died. I wondered how they knew. God's will or not, ALL feelings should be validated and allowed. This is part of grief, to question, to struggle, to be angry and sad. Also a part of grief is walking through and synthesizing new meaning, but this takes time—a lot of time. The people who help the most are those who humbly listen and love you no matter how nutty you sound. It is so important to develop support systems and to ask for help when you need it.

In the midst of the black clouds of grief, Dave and I also tried to provide the love and support that Michael needed. Michael was with us. We loved him more than ever and clearly knew what a wonderful gift a child is. We needed him. He needed us. He helped us pick ourselves up. He was the spark of life, our reason for living. Shortly after the funeral, we decided to take a family trip to the Roanoke Transportation Museum. As I snapped the picture of Dave and Michael in front of the steam locomotive, I wept for the little one who would never again be in our pictures. For a long time, I pined for the All-American Family with two kids, a dog, and a house in the suburbs—the whole bit. Our values were challenged.

On Michael's last day of nursery school just one month after Thomas died, I went to the customary ice cream festival. While sitting next to Michael appreciating being alive and rather enjoying my son and my sundae, a woman came up to a friend of mine within earshot and said, "Where is the one whose baby died?" There were nervous glances. Here I am, I thought. I'm sure her day was ruined, too. These days were hard. They were part of the grief.

One evening I found my way to the Compassionate Friends meeting in Virginia Baptist Hospital. At first, I felt awkward, like I didn't quite fit in. Over time, I found many new friends, friends who did not tell me how I "should" feel, friends who weren't surprised or embarrassed by a sudden flow of tears. The group was to become an important link to recovery.

The warm carefree days of summer arrived, a summer without anniversary dates. Grief was easier to bear on these barefoot days. Then bittersweet October rolled around—the birthdays of both our boys. Memories of Thomas. A party for Michael. In November, the flood waters rose, leaving behind devastation for many area families. I felt a small bit of their anguish with greater empathy than ever before. In December, I opened the box of Christmas ornaments and was unprepared to find the angel ornament which said "Baby's First Christmas" that my parents had given Thomas the year before. Misty-eyed, I sang carols with Michael. Life goes on.

Driving past Charlottesville brought fresh tears, memories of our hospital home, and the friends we made there. January through April were the darkest months of all. The winter chilled me to the core. The earth was barren. I struggled and cursed God for my plight. Why? Why us? We had so much to offer our children; and, what's more, we freely chose to have two children. I was certain that I never would accept this injustice.

It seemed that the winter would never end. But it was that very winter that poetry began to pour from my heart in the middle of sleepless, tormented nights. *Healing* sprang from my inner well, longing to be free. Almost without conscious effort, the words spilled onto the paper. One. Then another. And another. At first, I guarded my words with my life, taking care that prying eyes not intrude. One day after writing many, I decided to let my very best friends in on my frenzied musings, my secret self. They cried. They were moved. I felt understood. So much had happened that did not meet the eye. I wanted people to understand. Yes! This is my way. I know it. Once again, the die was cast.

I reopened my cherished copy of *A Grief Observed*. After C. S. Lewis' wife died from cancer, he found peace in a journal. He wrote:

What would H. herself think of this terrible notebook to which I come back and back? Are these jottings morbid? . . . But what am I to do? I must have some drug, and reading isn't a strong enough drug now. By writing it all down (all? no; one thought in a hundred) I believe I get a little outside it. (8)

Yes, I agree. I, too, must write. Writing releases the tears; it helps me move through the pain. Yes, my child is dead. Dead. Dead. Dead. I've said the word that we, in America, hate to say or hear. There is nothing I can do to change it. I've paid my dues, and I will rediscover joy in my life and find meaning in spite of this tragedy. Perhaps I should say BECAUSE of this crisis, my life from this point onward will be different. I will NEVER be the same person, and that doesn't have to be all bad. I began to see movement. Once again, there was hope. . . .

When I grieve in your presence,
I open a window to my soul.
The turbulence,
   the thrashing,
      the tears,
         the bitterness
will not destroy me . . .
unless they are forced inside.

Help me get the pain out
by being patient,
   by listening,
      by showing me with your eyes . . .
that you'll weather the storm.

Please do not say too much,
just let me be.
I'll show you the way,
then, rejoice with me
when I can laugh and play again . . .
for you are a catalyst
in my learning to live again.

3/9/86

6

A NEW BEGINNING

After long anticipation, the one-year anniversary of Thomas' death came and went. Once again, the days became warm and sunny. The burden of fresh grief lifted. Ever so gradually, I felt myself reentering the mainstream of life. I dug, clipped, and mulched in the yard with Michael. I opened the front door to take in the view of life and nature. I watched birds in the birdbath with delight and wonderment. Some of my old self returned, along with some new awarenesses and behaviors.

As I reflect on it, I know that I decided to choose life. I began to see that while there are those who love and care for us, we must learn to stand alone. No one else holds the key for my happiness.

I began to ask existential questions. Who am I really? What is my purpose in life? I began the road to recovery, realizing that it will be a life-long process. I believe that the pain of any major loss will continue to rear its head from time to time, but I will continue to manage it and process its significance to my life.

I am a different person now. I see things that I'd never seriously thought about before. Obituaries of other fathers, mothers, babies and children. The shuttle explosion of 1986 in the context of the raw pain of the families left behind. The stark reality of AIDS. Chernobyl. Pictures of missing children on milk cartons. In spite of the devastation all around me, there is a richness and quality to life that I want to grasp and cling to.

Now I really see the other parents in meetings of Compassionate Friends who hurt so deeply. The purpose of this self-help group for bereaved parents has become crystal clear to me. In that room each month is living proof that we, as individuals, weren't singled out for torture. The message that survival is possible is apparent from the parents who have moved along in the grief process and are now able to smile again and to help those just beginning the journey. It is hard work to reconstruct a new identity after a major loss, but it is possible. We have to make the choice and then be very patient with ourselves. We fall many times.

As the days have passed, I have become more involved with life and living. I have reinvested my energy in new projects. Elisabeth Kübler-Ross' words, "Dying is easy, living is hard," return to me over and over again, as I give myself permission to make mistakes and fail. I take more risks now.

Writing this book and these poems and sharing them with others is a new endeavor for me. Thomas gave me the story that needed to be written. Many times the writing brought up incredible pain, so much so that I had to lay my pen down for much-needed respite. But the urgings deep inside always brought me back. Initially, I began the project as a form of working through my own powerful feelings of grief. If my sharing touches someone else in some way, I am doubly enriched. In giving, I too receive.

It is difficult to put into words all that I've learned from Thomas, partly because my own feelings are dichotomous. I learned to love him, yet I've also learned to reconstruct my life without him. Then I wonder, "Did I not really love him?" I miss him, yet I know life would not have been easy had he lived. The doctors had told us he would need a heart valve replacement several years down the road. I wonder what he would be like now. Would I struggle and curse delays in developmental milestones? Or would I view each accomplishment with delight and euphoria? In seeing him as a unique human being would I be able to accept that he would do things at his own rate?

I am certain that I would do all of these things. I am human. I become impatient and irritable at times. Life is not fair, nor is it perfect. Neither am I. Somewhere in my journey, I became aware of my choices. I could spend the rest of my days bitter and angry over my plight. Or I could choose to forgive life, to remember that I am not the only one who has had pain. In forgiving, I opened the door to life and love and new possibilities. I feel rich again.

When Thomas died, I felt a sense of conclusion and relief that he would not continue to lie in a hospital bed for days on end. Yet I grieved bitterly, and still do at times. Grief no longer permeates my every thought and word, however. I have learned that we all grieve in one way or another. The circumstances may be different, but grief is a universal experience. Life is hard. There are successes. There are failures. There are many questions, few hard and fast answers.

A great deal of my learning from Thomas centers around the issue of unconditional acceptance, and in no way do I assume that my learning is complete. When we love and are loved without contingencies, this is the love that enriches our lives and frees us to reach our highest potential. I grew up playing with "perfect" Barbie dolls and seeing handsome Beatles on television. Thomas forced me to look at human variability; he planted the seeds of change. He taught me to look at differences, to see the person behind the label.

The words of Burton Blatt, the late Dean of the School of Education at Syracuse University and an ardent reformer in the field of developmental disabilities, further challenges my thinking:

The gifts that this movement [special education] was to endow us with were the gifts of optimism and belief in the human ethos, charity and love for our brothers, and the conviction that our work is not to judge who can or cannot change but rather to fulfill the prophecy that all people can change; each person can learn. For the promise to be kept, for these things to occur beyond wish or fantasy, one must begin with oneself. Before I ask the world to change, I must change. I am the beginning step. (9)

In the short months that Thomas lived with us, we saw him grow and learn. His learning was exciting to us. Recently, I accepted a position that that I probably never would have had if Thomas had not planted those seeds of change. I function as an advocate for persons with mental retardation. As I work with these clients, their disabilities become increasingly insignificant. Before Thomas, I never got past the label; today, I see people who do not fit into any clearly defined mold. They are people who laugh, cry, and do things in their own ways. They have strengths and weaknesses, as we all do. They, too, are teaching me about life. I also feel frustrated with them sometimes, as I have with my friends or family members.

Working with these special people has brought back the sense of mission that I lost when Thomas died. I see the needs of these people in our community for housing, education, medical care, recreation, transportation, employment, and most of all, acceptance and understanding from others. Their needs are many, and, as a society, we've only just begun to improve the quality of life for people with disabilities. In serving, my pain has greatly diminished. Through them, it is as though

Thomas lives on in my life, and that is a very good feeling. I remember the secrets he taught me. I do not want to forget.

In a special way, Thomas' life was perfect just as it was. His life touches us still in a dramatic way. A year-and-a-half after his death, I continue to discover what his life was all about. I continue to notice new intricacies in the fabric of life. I am more grateful for my health and the health of those I care about than ever before.

Admittedly, I am more vulnerable now. I know how quickly the tides of life can turn. The feelings of panic and fear come up when one of my loved ones is hurt or ill or a particular phrase or event reminds me of where we have been. I try not to dwell on our lack of control over our lives.

When we come face to face with our own mortality, we can choose to make the time we have richer. We learn that the sun doesn't shine forever; we learn to "make hay while the sun shines." Our middle-class complacency was stripped away. We looked at life through the eyes of a frightened animal about to meet its death. We will never be the same.

I am more aware of the passage of time now. As I look back over the tattered pages of my journal, I see new-found strength. There is light at the end of the tunnel. Michael is in kindergarten now. I love watching him grow and learn. I've learned to laugh again. Yes, I still cry. But I have purpose again. Dave, Michael, and Thomas, each in his own way, have taught me to see beauty in each season of life, even in winter which seems, at times, so barren and desolate.

Life flows onward. There are twists and turns. As we rejoice in all we have, we will feel sadness over what might have been. We will summon the strength to accept the unknowns of the other side of this life. I recall a passage which comforts me:

> Though I am dead, grieve not for me with tears, think not of death with sorrowing and tears. I am so near that every tear you shed touches and tortures me, though you think me dead. But when you laugh and sing in glad delight, my soul is lifted upward to the light. Laugh and be glad for all that life is giving and I, though dead, will share your joy in living. (10)

I have struggled for weeks to compose a closing for this book only to discover the obvious: there is no closing. The story lives as I grow and learn, as I approach the days of my life with the backdrop of having known and loved a child with special needs. This fact, I believe, will forevermore alter my approach to life. No longer will I turn away in embarrassment or fear. No longer will I stick my head in the sand and pretend that differences don't exist. Before I can ask the world to change, I must change. Behind the handicap is a person who, like me, is not perfect, but who, like me, responds to love and affirmation. When a child dies, I will not pretend that it did not happen. A family needs help then more than ever, a listening ear, not an advice-giver. A loving note. A wholesome dish of food. I am the beginning step. I have power. With this power goes the responsibility to use it wisely.

I am walking on now. With great pain comes new perspectives . . . when we learn to let go.

The End. . . .
A New Beginning. . . .

EPILOGUE

As a professor, one of my responsibilities is to convey factual information. Liz Farnsworth has asked me to do just that here. It was her concern that some readers of her book might not have had the opportunity to become acquainted with the basic information available about Down Syndrome. It is my pleasure to contribute to this book by reviewing some of the facts I have discussed so often with my students.

The term Down Syndrome is derived from the name of the first person who systematically studied and wrote about the condition, Dr. J. Langdon Down. A nineteenth century English physician, Down was actually the first to apply the term "mongoloid" to children born with this condition. He felt these children were reversions to a lower rung on the ladder of human evolution; he was actually arguing that when a child with Down Syndrome was born to Caucasian parents something had caused the fetus to revert to an Asian type. It is important that we all be aware that use of the term "mongoloid" is not only degrading to these children, it is racist as well.

Just over twenty-five years ago a French scientist, Dr. Jerome Lejune, discovered that Down Syndrome is caused by the presence of an extra chromosome in the cells of persons with the condition. People with Down Syndrome have forty-seven chromosomes instead of the usual forty-six found in most human cells. The forty-six chromosomes which most of us have are arranged into twenty-three pairs within each cell. In the case of Down Syndrome the extra chromosome is attached to pair #21. For this reason the condition is sometimes referred to as "Trisomy 21." Down Syndrome is present from the time of conception. When the egg and sperm unite, the extra chromosome is there. Faulty cell division in the production of the egg or sperm has left more chromosomal material in the cell than is usually the case at conception. There are two variations which cause more rare forms of Down Syndrome, but Trisomy 21 is by far the most common form of the disorder.

Down Syndrome occurs once in every six or seven hundred live births. The birth of a child with Down Syndrome is not, therefore, as aberrant an event as is sometimes thought in the general population. It is the single most common cause of mental retardation in newborns. This reality makes even more important the message that Liz Farnsworth has brought to us through this book.

Children with Down Syndrome may be born with a number of possible physical characteristics. They often have poor muscle tone and weak reflexes. The tongue may appear large and deeply fissured. Hair may be coarse and sparse. One identifying characteristic is a special crease across the palm of the hand. The eyes may slant slightly upward. With all due respect to J. Langdon Down, however, they do not look Asian. Check for yourself; it will impress upon you the inaccuracy of the use of the unfortunate term "mongoloid."

People with Down Syndrome are particularly subject to respiratory infections. Before the development of modern medication for treating respiratory problems, this vulnerability was a much more serious concern and was a significant factor in the high infant and child mortality rate among Down Syndrome children.

Heart problems, as we have come to know so vividly from this book, pose a survival threat to many of these youngsters. More than a third of all of these children have some type of congenital heart defect. Even with today's advanced diagnostic and surgical capabilities, heart defects are still a major cause of early death for children with Down Syndrome.

We do not yet understand how the physical characteristics and problems described above are caused by Trisomy 21. Likewise, we do not understand why Down Syndrome is usually accompanied by mental retardation. I say usually because there have been cases recorded of Down Syndrome individuals with normal intelligence. Most commonly, however, Down Syndrome people function within the moderate range of mental retardation. With the growth and development of early intervention programs, there are growing numbers of these children who eventually function within the mild level of retardation. It is most important, however, that we remember that people with Down Syndrome are individuals who develop in this world, like the rest of the human family, in different ways, to different capacities, with different needs, and expressing different talents.

And so I have presented some factual information. I presented these facts to Liz Farnsworth when she took my introductory course on the nature and needs of special children. I remember how we explored and discussed these facts as professor and graduate student. I recall her enthusiasm and maturity as we examined, in our academic context, the creation of "special families" by the unexpected arrival of a child with exceptional needs.

The next time we spoke of Down Syndrome, it was not as professor and student but as friends. Through Thomas I came to know Liz as I had not known her before. He gave us the opportunity to share tears, fears, and hope. He gave me the chance to see Dave Farnsworth's gentleness and devotion as a father and husband. He let me see Michael's remarkable understanding and compassion. I treasure these glimpses of love, commitment, and wisdom.

In his book *Journey*, Robert Massie describes Charles DeGaulle as one of those famous people who grow larger, instead of smaller, as more is learned of them as parents. Even in the midst of his heaviest involvement in war, politics, and world affairs, he apparently always found time to spend with his daughter, Anne, who had Down Syndrome. Massie reports that DeGaulle was never too busy to bring a smile to his daughter's face with his songs and dances. When Anne was born, DeGaulle's wife Yvonne wrote, "Charles and I would give everything: health, fortune, promotion, career, if only Anne were a little girl like the others." When Anne died, DeGaulle stood by the grave, took his wife's hand and said, "Come, now she is like the others" (11).

Thomas became "like the others" before his death. Through the love and acceptance of his family, he found his place and his value as a human being. He also retained his "specialness," however, and became a teacher. As Liz has portrayed in this book, the lessons he taught were profound and lasting.

In 1886, Randolph Bourne's face was permanently damaged by the forceps used at his birth. When he was only four years old, spinal tuberculosis caused a twisting of his spine. He was, as a result of that illness, to be left short and hunchbacked. He endured a childhood and adolescence characterized by stigma and prejudice because of his disabilities. Later, however, he found a supportive social group that accepted him, earned a college degree, and became a respected writer. He also became known as a social reformer with a particular interest in children and education.

From his own suffering, Randolph Bourne learned a "profound sympathy for all who are despised and ignored in the world ... for the unpresentable and the unemployable, the incompetent and the ugly, the queer and the crotchety people who make up so large a proportion of human folk" (12). "He learned to find the unsuccessful as interesting as the successful, to see the world through the eyes of the struggling many rather than those of the fortunate few, to imagine and work for a social order in which there was more joy and less inequality" (13).

Bourne felt that his disabilities had made him sensitive in ways that he may not have been otherwise. He explained: "It is hard to tell just how much of this philosophy has been due to my handicaps. If it is solely to my physical misfortunes that I owe its existence, the price has not been a heavy one to pay. For it has given me something I would not know how to be without" (14).

Thomas gave something to his family that they would not now know how to be without. Through writing this book, Liz Farnsworth has shared with us part of that "something." I think it can be an important gift for any reader. I hope, however, that it will reach some people who face challenges similar to those that Liz has here described.

In her book, *A Difference in the Family*, Helen Featherstone quotes Claire and Joseph Canning. The Cannings, parents of a daughter with Down Syndrome, have written that their grief would have been more bearable "if just one person had come to tell us that despite our sadness there was hope, that this was not the end of the world, but rather a challenge . . ." (15). Liz Farnsworth has offered up a story of sadness and of hope. I hope it will reach some of those who most need it.

John David Smith, Ed.D.
Professor of Education & Human Development
Lynchburg College
Lynchburg, Virginia

July, 1987

POEMS

Reaching out again
feels awkward.
Like a newborn bird
testing its wings,
I am frightened.
I need practice at living again.

Grief has left me . . .
        weary,
        empty,
        lonely,
        unsure
        AGAIN.

Grief strips away the familiar
and leaves one a stranger
in a foreign land
        FOR A WHILE.

As a bird's wings are made for
flight,
so the human is made to grow.

Try again. . .
Another false start.
Soon I will soar
up where the air is fresh and
clean.

Life knocks us down.
        WE CAN GET UP.

We were given minds
to create meaning,
to weather the windstorms of life.

NO, it is not easy.
Yet, like the baby bird
I must try again.
Little by little
strength is restored.
Healing comes gradually.

I can live again
to sense all the wonders
and beauty of life . . .
to give back to life
with greater depth and sensitivity
and learn that there is purpose
        EVEN IN GRIEF.

        2/14/86

LIGHT

Today my son and I
flung open the front door
and just sat and
basked in the light
of the sun.

After days on end
of rain and clouds,
it was lovely . . .
just to bask in the light
of the sun.

One of the greatest teachings of tragedy
is to learn to appreciate
just what you have,
not lust for more
. . . to realize there's no promise of tomorrow
and to just be content to sit
and bask in the light of the sun.

2/21/86

I REMEMBER THOMAS

When I feel like giving up,
I remember Thomas.
When the path seems too rocky
and I contemplate retreating,
I remember Thomas.

As I view the sparkling lights of Christmas,
how can I not remember him?
He was my son. He had Down Syndrome.
Why MY son? He was not the child I expected,
yet I learned to appreciate his giggles, his coos,
his gentle way.

When the silent snowflakes fall,
then, too, I will remember him.
He was not perfect, nor am I.
Nor are you.

When the spring rains nourish the life of the earth,
I will remember him.
He was my teacher. He made me take a stand.

In summer, as I watch the tide roll in,
I will remember him.
He taught me that what I feel is RIGHT . . . for me.
Feelings come and feelings go.
In acknowledging them, we learn to let go.

As the leaves turn in October, his birth month,
I will wonder about what might have been.
In a wonderful way, he released me
from the bondage of . . . myself.
He taught me to keep reaching . . . upward
. . . toward the LIGHT.

Finite . . . yet timeless . . . we all are.
Crises transform us to a new time and place
. . . when we learn to let go.
Sometimes I will grieve for former times.
Other times, in glad delight, I will rejoice
in who I've become.

In standing alone, we learn that we are never alone.
LIFE flows on . . . infinitely.

In all that I am,
all that I do,
I will always remember Thomas.

12/24/86

NOTES

1. Brazelton, T. B. *Infants and Mothers - Differences in Development.* New York: Delacorte Press, 1983.

2. Dmitriev, V. *Time to Begin: Early Education for Children With Down Syndrome.* Available through Caring, P.O. Box 400, Milton, WA 98354. 1982.

3. Cunningham, C., & Sloper, P. *Helping Your Exceptional Baby.* New York: Pantheon Books, 1980.

4. The author wishes to express appreciation to Fred M. Rogers for granting permission to use this quote in this book.

5. Jablow, M. M. *CARA.* Philadelphia, PA: Temple University Press, 1983.

6. Lewis, C. S. *A Grief Observed.* New York: Bantam Books, 1961, p. 89.

7. Kubler-Ross, E. *Death: The Final Stage of Growth.* Englewood Cliffs, NJ: Prentice-Hall, 1975, p. 73.

8. Lewis, C. S. *A Grief Observed.* New York: Bantam Books, 1961, p. 9–10.

9. Blatt, B. *In & Out of Mental Retardation.* Baltimore: University Park Press, 1981.

10. Stephens, S. *Death Comes Home.* London: A. R. Mowbray & Co. Ltd., 1973, p. 108.

11. Massie, R. and Massie, S. *Journey.* New York: Alfred A. Knopf, 1975, p. 407.

12. Bourne, R. "The Handicapped." *Atlantic Monthly.* 1911. 108 (Sept.), p. 321.

13. Featherstone, H. *A Difference in the Family.* New York: Basic Books, 1980, p. 240.

14. Bourne, R. "The Handicapped." *Atlantic Monthly.* 1911. 108 (Sept.), p. 327.

15. Canning, J. and Canning, C. *The Gift of Martha.* Children's Hospital Medical Center (1975) as cited in Featherstone, H. *A Difference in the Family.* New York: Basic Books, 1980, p. 9.

RESOURCE LIST

*Abbott, S. (1972). *Old dog*. NY: Coward, McCann & Geoghegen.

*Anders, R. (1978). *A look at death*. Minneapolis: Lerner.

Bloomfield, H., M. Colgrove & P. McWilliams. (1976). *How to survive the loss of a love*. NY: Bantam.

Bluebond-Langner,M. (1978) *The private worlds of dying children*. NJ: Princeton University Press.

Bordow, J. (1982). *The ultimate loss*. NY: Beaufort Books.

*Brown, M.W. (1958). *The dead bird*. Reading, MA: Addison-Wesley.

*Buck, P. *The big wave*. NY: Scholastic Book Service.

*Buscaglia, L. (1982). *The fall of Freddie the leaf*. NJ: Charles B. Slack, Inc.

*Carrick, C. (1976). *The accident*. NY: Seabury.

*Craven, M. (1973). *I heard the owl call my name*. NY: Doubleday.

D'Arcy, P. (1979). *Song for Sarah*. Wheaton, IL: Harold Shaw.

D'Arcy, P. (1984). *Where the wind begins*. Wheaton, IL: Harold Shaw.

Deford, F. (1983). *Alex: The life of a child*. NY: Viking.

Donnelly, K. (1982). *Recovering from the loss of a child*. NY: Macmillan.

*Fassler, J. (1971). *My grandpa died today*. NY: Behavioral Publications.

Grollman, E. A. (1981). *What helped me when my loved one died*. Boston: Beacon Press.

Grollman, E. A. (1977). *Living when a loved one has died*. Boston: Beacon Press.

*Grollman, E. A. (1971). *Talking about death: A dialogue between parent and child*. Boston: Beacon Press.

Gunther, J. (1949). *Death be not proud*. NY: Harper & Row.

Jones, W. (1977) "Death-related grief counseling: The school counselor's responsibility." *School Counselor*, 24, 315–320.

*Kaplan, B. (1978). *The empty chair*. NY: Harper.

*Klein, N. (1974). *Confessions of an only child*. NY: Pantheon.

Kotzwinkel, W. (1981). *Swimmer in the secret sea*. NY: Avon.

Kreis, B. & A. Pattie. (1969). *Up from grief*. Minneapolis: Winston Press.

*Krementz, J. (1981). *How it feels when a parent dies: Children of sorrow.* NY: Alfred A. Knopf.

Kübler-Ross, E. (1983). *On children and death.* NY: Macmillan.

Kübler-Ross, E. (1982). *Working it through.* NY: Macmillan.

Kübler-Ross, E. (1975). *Death: The final stage of growth.* NJ: Prentice-Hall.

Kübler-Ross, E. (1969). *On death and dying.* NY: Macmillan.

Kushner, H.S. (1981). *When bad things happen to good people.* NY: Avon.

LaTour, K. (1983). *For those who live.* Dallas: LaTour.

*LeShan, E. (1976). *Learning to say goodbye: When a parent dies.* NY: Macmillan.

Lewis, C.S. (1961). *A grief observed.* NY: Bantam.

Lovern, P. et. al. (1981). *Our child died.* Lynchburg, Va.: by Virginia Baptist Hospital.

*Mann, P. (1977). *There are two kinds of terrible.* NY: Doubleday.

*Mellonie, B. and R. Ingpen. (1983). *Lifetimes.* NY: Bantam.

Miller, W. A. (1976). *When going to pieces holds you together.* Minneapolis: Augsburg.

*Paterson, K. (1977). *Bridge to Terabithia.* NY: Crowell.

*Peck, R.N. (1972). *A day no pigs would die.* NY: Dell.

*Richter, E. (1986). *Losing someone you love: When a brother or sister dies*. NY: G.T. Putnam's Sons.

*Rofes, E.E. (1985). *The kids' book about death and dying*. Boston: Little, Brown and Co.

Schiff, H.S. (1977). *The bereaved parent*. NY: Penguin.

*Simon, N. (1979). *We remember Phillip*. Chicago: Whitman.

*Sims, A.M. (1986). *Am I still a sister?* Order from A. Sims, Box 20882, Albuquerque, NM 87154.

*Smith, D. (1973). *A taste of blackberries*. NY: Scholastic.

*Stein, S.B. (1974). *About dying: An open book for parents and children together*. NY: Walker & Co.

Stephens, S. (1973). *Death comes home*. NY: Morehouse-Barlow.

Stinson, P. and R. Stinson. (1983). *The long dying of baby Andrew*. Boston: Little, Brown and Co.

*Viorst, J. (1971). *The tenth good thing about Barney*. NY: Atheneum.

Westburg, G.E. (1962). *Good grief*. Philadelphia: Fortress Press.

*White, E.B. (1952). *Charlotte's web*. NY: Harper & Row.

Wolf, A.W.M. (1973). *Helping your child to understand death*. NY: Child Study Press.

Worden, J. W. (1982). *Grief counseling and grief therapy*. NY: Springer.

*books for children.